MW01516306

in Modern
Science

Power
Ethical Debates about Resources and the Environment

BY KATE RAVILIOUS

Contents

⬤ Introduction 6

⬤ Environmental Ethics 8

⬤ Power and Energy 12

⬤ Renewable Resources 20

⬤ Transportation and Travel 28

⬤ Wood and Water 34

⬤ The Environment and You 38

⬤ Time Line 42

⬤ More Information 43

⬤ Glossary 44

⬤ Index 46

Introduction

Humans are pushing the boundaries of science and technology. We can access information at the touch of a button. We can genetically modify food so it grows faster and tastes better. We have developed medicines that can cure once-fatal illnesses. All this might sound positive, but we are now facing many dilemmas in the areas of science, technology, and medicine. Just because we *can* do something, does this mean we *should*?

Many of these debates are based on what is ethically or morally right—for humans, for animals, or for the environment. People often feel very strongly about such issues, whether they are governments, special interest groups, or individuals. It is important for everyone to understand what these ethical questions are and to consider the ways in which they might be solved.

What Are Natural Resources?

How we use the Earth's natural resources is one of the most controversial points of debate in the twenty-first century. So why are they so important, and how has their use come into question?

One of the first uses of natural resources was making fire by rubbing sticks together.

Wind, water, trees, sunshine, coal, oil, gas, minerals, and gemstones—these are just some of the natural resources provided by our planet and our solar system. All living things rely on resources; most animals could not survive without water, plants, sunshine, and fresh air. Humans depend on these and other resources more than any other creature.

It all started thousands of years ago when humans first discovered fire. They gradually learned to use resources to help control their environment and become a successful species. Somewhere between 5,000 and 10,000 years ago, people began to grow crops, which enabled them to settle in one place. Most of these early people managed to live in balance with the Earth, replenishing the resources as they were used up or moving on when they ran out.

By the early nineteenth century, the Industrial Revolution was in full swing. Steam power (fueled by coal), machinery, railways, roads, and canals transformed the way people lived, leading to mass production of goods and an improved standard of living for many. Suddenly humans started to use up resources at a tremendous pace. Entire forests were cut down, coal seams were mined, hillsides quarried, and gallons of water flushed down the drain. This rapid consumption has continued to the present day.

The Industrial Revolution of the nineteenth century resulted in natural resources such as coal being used at a much greater rate than ever before. The steam traction engine, used in farming, was one of many technological developments from this period.

Globalization

Within the last few decades, technologies such as the telephone, air travel, and the Internet have led to globalization. Our warm homes, fully stocked supermarkets, and satellite television all rely on a global chain of resources. One break in that chain, such as a power cut or fuel shortage, can lead to severe disruption. We all depend on resources and the distribution network that moves them around the world.

Today, some natural resources are growing scarce. If we do not plan ahead, our civilization could collapse. There is a pressing need for all people to look at the way they live and decide who controls these resources, how best to use them, and how to share them fairly.

1 Environmental Ethics

Not everyone holds the same view about how the environment should be treated and its resources shared. This has led to the formation of a number of organizations that represent different viewpoints and fight for the causes they believe in.

In 1962, Rachel Carson, an American zoologist and marine biologist, published a book called *Silent Spring*, which highlighted the dangers of pesticides and the threat they pose to wildlife, especially birds. The book was highly controversial at the time, but it alerted people to the fragility of the Earth's environment and the damage that modern living can inflict.

Special Interest Groups

By the late 1960s and early 1970s, a number of environmental groups had been formed, campaigning for sustainable management of resources and care for the Earth's environment. Some of those groups, such as the international organizations Greenpeace and Earth Day Network, are still active today. They organize campaigns and protests, and carry out research to find new solutions.

The groups vary in how confrontational their actions are. Greenpeace uses direct action. Members do things such as chaining themselves to trees to stop them from being cut down, or using the Greenpeace ship *Rainbow Warrior* to get in the way of whaling boats. Friends of the Earth in the United Kingdom (the UK) and Earth Day Network usually take a less direct approach and try to get their message across with street protests and educational events. These actions are different ways of expressing opinions about the ethical issues surrounding resources and the environment.

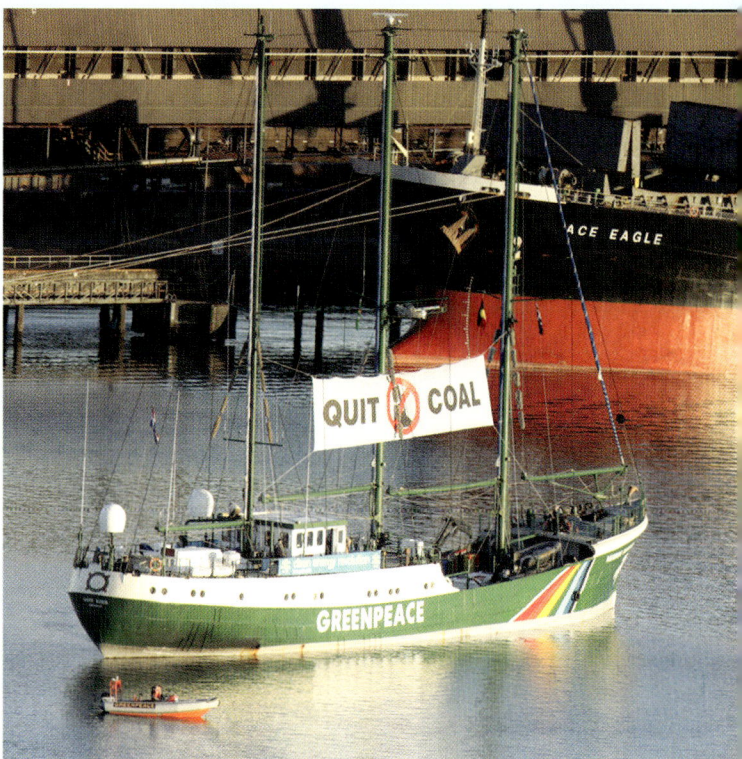

The Greenpeace ship Rainbow Warrior *blocks a coal ship in the Australian port of Newcastle. Groups like Greenpeace take disruptive action in their campaigns against the use of Earth's resources.*

Scientist James Lovelock, whose Gaia hypothesis was one of the earliest suggestions that humans were interfering with the natural balance of the environment.

Gaia Theory

Prominent scientists can also influence the way people think about ethical issues. James Lovelock, a British scientist, is famous for the Gaia hypothesis. This is the idea that the Earth behaves as if it were a living organism, where factors like the saltiness of the sea, the amount of oxygen in the air, and the cloudiness of the sky are all interacting processes. He has proposed that these processes regulate each other and keep everything in balance. Humans have damaged this balance by overusing resources and filling the atmosphere with greenhouse gases. Lovelock suggests this imbalance is like a disease affecting Gaia, which has brought the Earth to the brink of a crisis.

❝ *When the last tree is cut, the last river poisoned, and the last fish dead, we will discover that we can't eat money…* ❞

Greenpeace banner

YOU DECIDE

In September 2006, Greenpeace activists chained themselves to a pier at Map Ta Phut in Thailand and delayed the unloading of a shipment of Australian coal for a new power station in Thailand.

? The activists argued that the power plant will cause climate change and that Thailand will become reliant on Australian coal, instead of investing in renewable energy projects. Are these valid reasons for their actions?

? Should people be allowed to demonstrate their feelings in such a direct and disruptive way?

? Is direct action like this the best way to get a message across, or can less direct action, such as a street march, be equally effective?

Taking Action

Not everyone agrees with Gaia theory, but it has revolutionized the way people look at the environment and the effect their own actions can have. Some businesses are responding to public concerns and trying to be more responsible about the way they use the Earth's resources.

In September 2006, British billionaire businessman Sir Richard Branson announced that he would use all the profits from his Virgin air and railway businesses to fight global warming. Around $3 billion over the next 10 years will be invested in a new business venture, Virgin Fuels, which will research more environmentally friendly fuels.

Meanwhile, some politicians and policy makers are forcing people to change their ways. In the European Union, countries such as Denmark and Germany tax people according to what they throw away. Waste that can be recycled is removed free of charge, but every pound of rubbish that needs to go to a landfill or be incinerated, must be paid for.

Critics of Richard Branson's Virgin Fuels venture point out that technology will have to advance dramatically before planes can fly on biofuel. They also say that such investment discourages individuals from changing their own behavior and makes them think they can rely on science to solve the problem.

Many European countries, including Germany, insist on the recycling of household waste, making individuals play a part in helping the environment.

New laws in Massachusetts have been introduced to limit greenhouse-gas emissions from traffic.

> 66 *Unfortunately, much of current energy policy is driven by fears of global warming. It has led to undue emphasis on wind and solar power, on biofuels such as ethanol, and on schemes to sequester [capture] the CO_2 emitted from power plants.* 99
>
> *Science and Environmental Policy Project, 2006*

Environmental Politics

In the United States, some states are no longer waiting for the federal government to act. Instead, they are bringing in their own environmental laws. For example, California, Massachusetts, Oregon, and Connecticut, among others, have all recently passed bills that will force industries to reduce their greenhouse-gas emissions and help curb global warming. Such laws are often a response to the desires of the public to address ethical issues.

Not everyone is convinced that humans are destroying the environment, though, or that the Earth is under threat. Groups such as the Heritage Foundation in the U.S. and the Scientific Alliance in the UK try to counterbalance the opinions coming from certain environmental special interest groups. However, these organizations are sometimes criticized for accepting large sums of money from businesses such as oil and mining companies, which have a vested interest in using the Earth's natural resources. This has raised the question of whether their opinions are ethical or driven by financial incentives.

YOU DECIDE

The Heritage Foundation is financially supported by a number of corporations, including Chevron Texaco, ExxonMobil, and General Motors. Some of the findings made by the Heritage Foundation have influenced environmental policy in the United States.

❓ *Is it right for special interest groups to accept funding from corporations?*

❓ *Is there a danger that this kind of funding might bias the opinions of an organization?*

❓ *Are any sources of funding truly unbiased?*

2 Power and Energy

Everything humans do needs energy—smiling, frowning, baking a cake, or sending an astronaut into space. The amount of energy powered by the Earth's natural resources has become a matter of increasing concern over the past few decades. Scientists are now trying to find ways of improving energy efficiency. One of the most important steps toward this goal is convincing people to change the way they use energy in their everyday lives.

Conservation of Energy

Energy never disappears; it simply changes from one form to another. For example, the human body converts food into power, which is used for movement. A car burns gasoline, converting the stored chemical energy into motion, heat, and noise—all forms of energy.

In the case of a car, more than half of the energy from burning the fuel is turned into heat and sound. A car has low energy efficiency because so much of the energy is converted into a form that we cannot put to good use. Energy efficiency is a measure of how much useful energy a device produces. In general, cars have less than 50 percent energy efficiency.

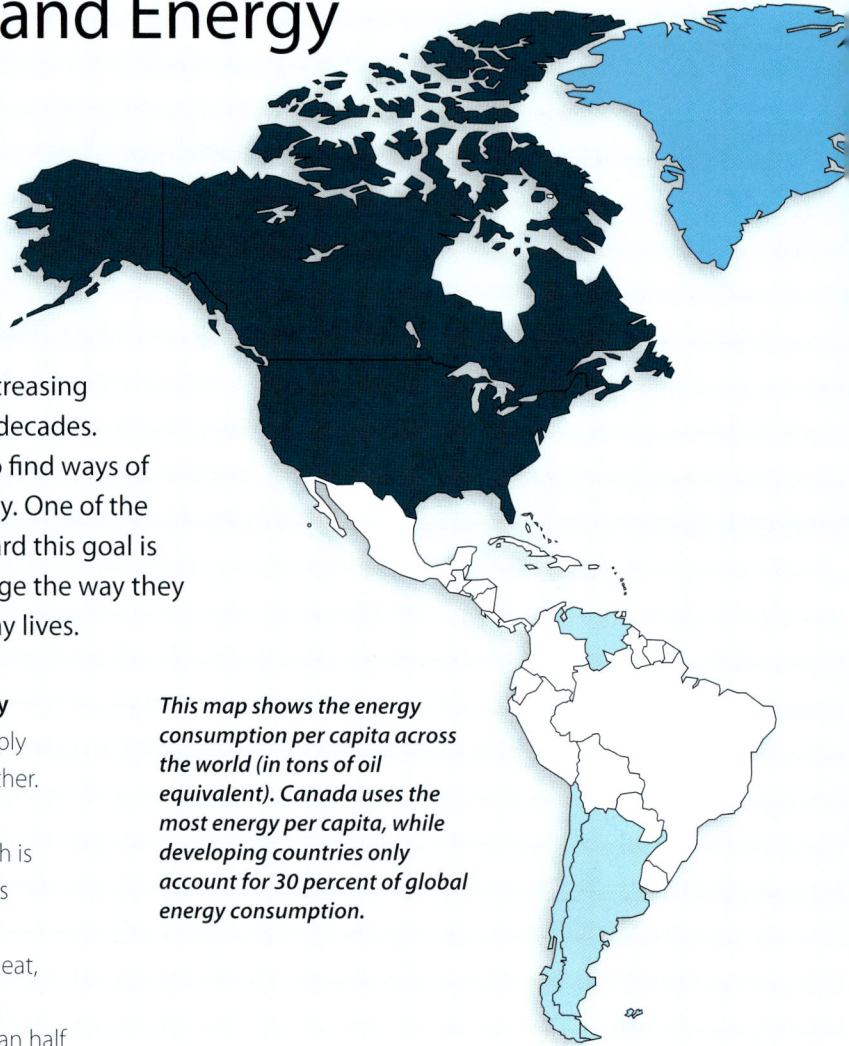

This map shows the energy consumption per capita across the world (in tons of oil equivalent). Canada uses the most energy per capita, while developing countries only account for 30 percent of global energy consumption.

> **An American uses six times as much energy, mostly fossil fuels, as the worldwide average, and 70 times more than a Bangladeshi. That same American consumes twice as much energy as do Western Europeans and three times as much as do Japanese.**

Norman Myers and Jennifer Kent
Perverse Subsidies

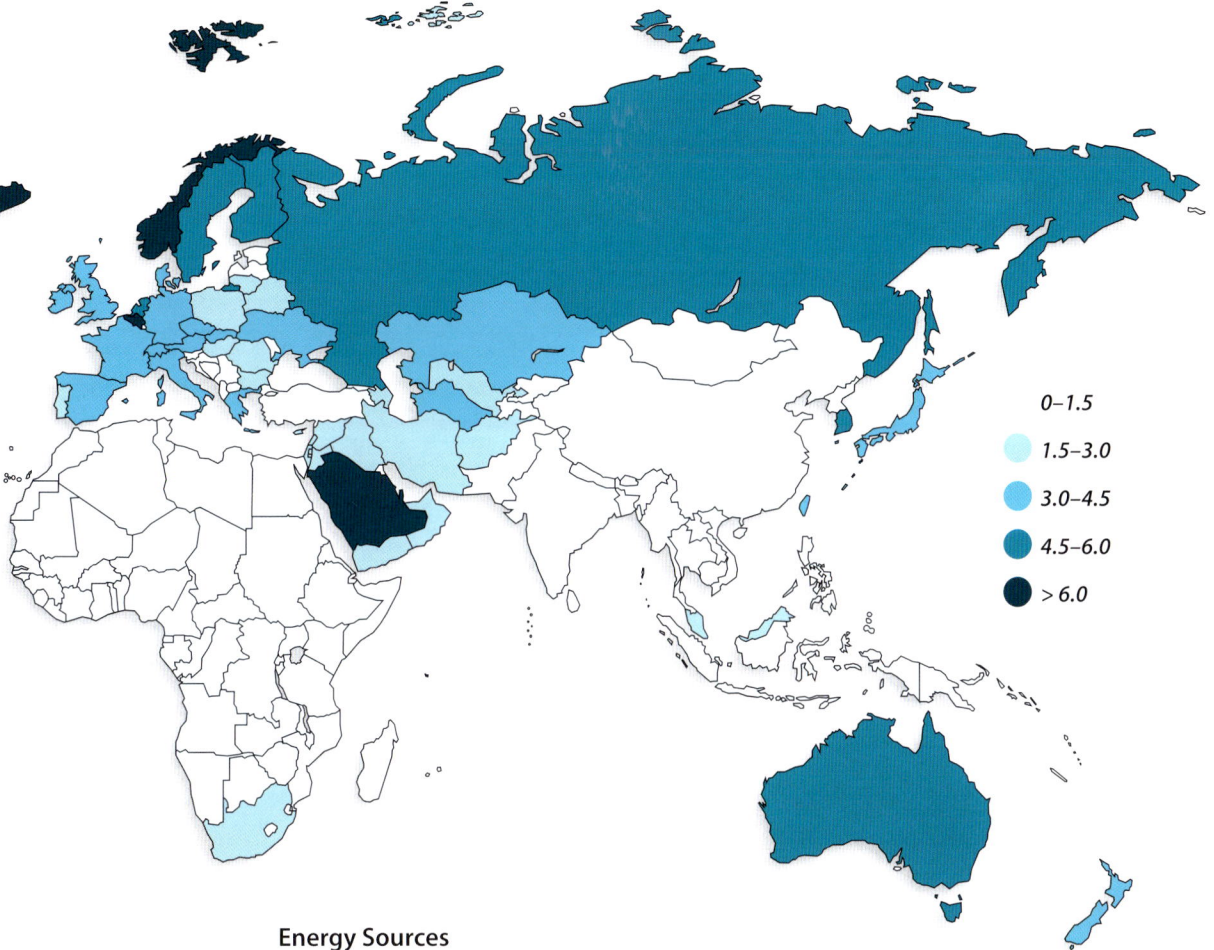

	0–1.5
	1.5–3.0
	3.0–4.5
	4.5–6.0
	> 6.0

Energy Sources

The energy we use falls into two groups: renewable and nonrenewable. Renewable energy sources are those that can be replenished at the same rate they are used. These include wind, wave, and solar power. Nonrenewable energy sources are used faster than we can replace them, such as coal, oil, gas, and uranium.

To make life more convenient, we sometimes make what are called "secondary" sources of energy. These help us store, move, and deliver energy in an easy-to-use form. Electricity and hydrogen are examples of secondary energy sources. In most developed countries, houses, offices, stores, and other buildings are connected to a power grid. This carries electricity from a power station along a system of power lines to homes and workplaces.

TYPES OF ENERGY

There are two types of energy: kinetic and potential. Kinetic energy is the energy of motion. Anything that is moving has kinetic energy: electrons moving along a wire, molecules jiggling inside a crystal , or light traveling from the Sun. Potential energy is energy that is stored and waiting to be converted into power, such as the water sitting behind a dam, molecular bonds inside a lump of coal, or the power inside a stretched rubber band.

13

Fossil Fuels

Finding ways of harnessing and controlling different forms of energy has transformed our lives. In particular, fossil fuels (coal, oil, and gas) have had a huge effect. These energy-rich substances were created millions of years ago from the remains of plants and animals (fossils) that were heated and compressed inside the Earth. Today we use them to enable us to live in cold places, travel huge distances, and communicate with people on the other side of the world. Fossil fuels supply 80 percent of the world's energy needs, but they are diminishing fast. Once they are gone, they cannot be replaced. One of the greatest ethical dilemmas facing us today is how to manage fossil-fuel consumption.

A Convenient Source of Energy

The beauty of fossil fuels is their convenience. They are relatively easy to move around and the energy stays locked up inside them until we are ready to use it. For example, coal can

FOSSIL-FUEL CONSUMPTION

Fossil fuels have been mined all over the world for centuries. However, scientists are now estimating that reserves of these fuels are running very low. The most optimistic estimates predict that coal will last another 252 years, gas 72 years, and oil just 32 years, if they continue to be used at the rate they are now.

Oil is one of the most useful fossil fuels. It is extracted from beneath the surface of the Earth using rigs like this. However, oil reserves are diminishing quickly.

Mining for coal is a dirty, difficult, and dangerous job. Using coal for energy also pumps pollutants into the atmosphere.

be mined in the U.S. and then shipped to Japan and used to power a blast furnace to make steel. Meanwhile, gas can be piped all the way from its source to your door, powering the central heating in your home and keeping you warm.

But there are problems with fossil fuels, too. They are nonrenewable and when used, release pollutants into the atmosphere that contribute to poor health and affect Earth's climate. Coal is particularly dirty and emits radioactive materials when it is burned.

Clean Coal Technology

Coal is one of the most polluting of all fossil fuels, but scientists have now developed a way of removing the impurities before it is burned, making the coal burn more efficiently. Once it has been burned, the smoke can be cleaned before it leaves the chimney, disposing of polluting gases such as sulphur dioxide.

One of the latest technologies is "carbon capture." This involves collecting carbon dioxide from power plants, before it can enter and damage the atmosphere, and storing it deep underground in places such as abandoned mines. Locking up carbon dioxide in this way will help combat global warming. However, capturing carbon dioxide uses significant amounts of energy. Some scientists are also concerned that the carbon dioxide may leak from its underground storage and end up polluting the atmosphere anyway.

YOU DECIDE

The Arctic National Wildlife Refuge lies in the northwest corner of Alaska. Many rare animal and bird species are found there, but the reserve is also valuable for its oil. There could be over 10 billion barrels of oil there, enough to power the U.S. for around two years. Extracting the oil may damage the environment.

? *In cases like this, should governments act in the best interests of people or the environment?*

? *Who does the oil belong to—the American people, the indigenous people who live on the refuge, or everyone?*

Greenhouse Gases

Carbon dioxide, water vapor, and methane are all examples of greenhouse gases. In the atmosphere they hold on to heat and create a warm blanket of air around the Earth. Without them the Earth's surface would be around 86°F (30°C) cooler, and most life forms would not be able to survive.

Volcanoes are a natural source of greenhouse gases, pumping them out each time they erupt. Meanwhile, plants and trees breathe in greenhouse gases when they photosynthesize, converting them into oxygen.

A Rapid Increase

Air samples which scientists have taken from bubbles inside ice cores show that the levels of carbon dioxide in the air have rocketed over the last 200 years. Before the Industrial Revolution, more than 200 years ago, carbon dioxide made up around 280 parts per million of air. By the year 2000, carbon dioxide made up 367 parts per million of air.

THE KYOTO PROTOCOL

The Kyoto Protocol is an agreement between a group of nations that commits them to reducing the amount of greenhouse gases produced by their countries. It sets targets for monitoring and achieving these reductions. As of July 2007, 175 countries had agreed to the Kyoto Protocol, covering more than half of the global greenhouse-gas emissions.

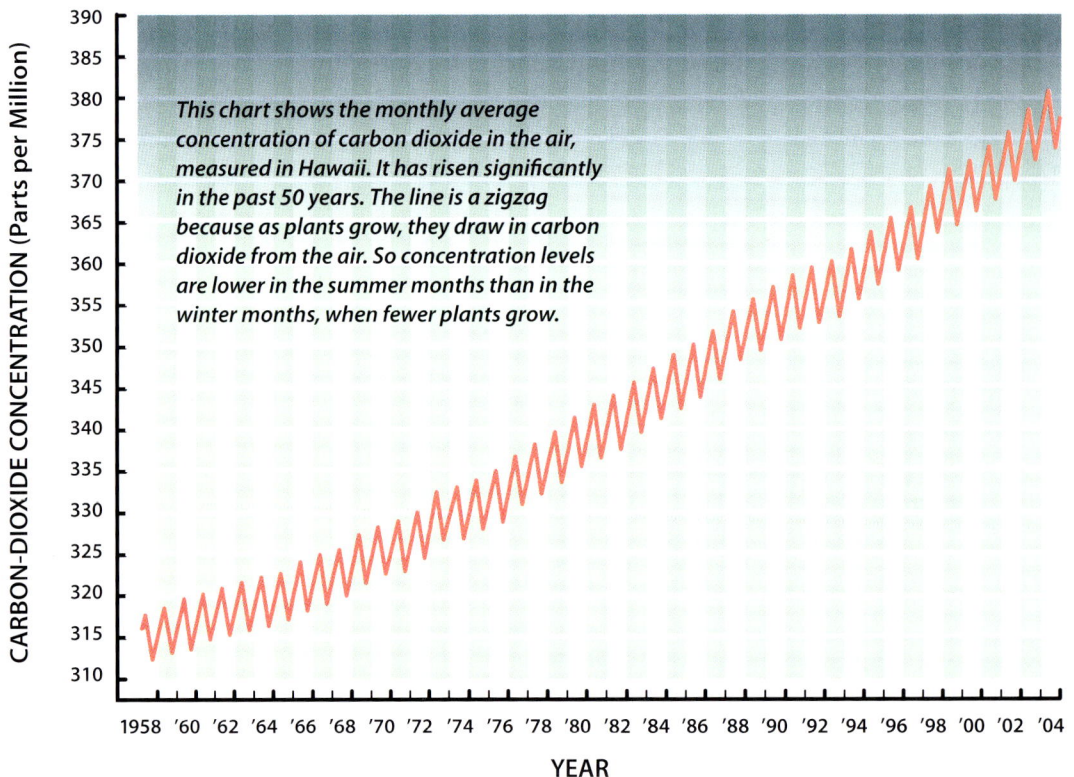

This chart shows the monthly average concentration of carbon dioxide in the air, measured in Hawaii. It has risen significantly in the past 50 years. The line is a zigzag because as plants grow, they draw in carbon dioxide from the air. So concentration levels are lower in the summer months than in the winter months, when fewer plants grow.

CARBON-DIOXIDE CONCENTRATION (Parts per Million)

YEAR

Burning fossil fuels for industry and cutting down trees which absorb carbon dioxide have caused much of this increase. Today, we are producing twice as much carbon dioxide as trees and plants can convert back into oxygen. This imbalance is causing huge problems for the environment and is an area of great debate among scientists and policy makers.

Warming Up

This thicker blanket of greenhouse gases is causing the planet to heat up. Over the last 100 years, the Earth's average surface temperature has risen by more than .9°F (.5°C). Already this small change has had a very dramatic effect. Global mean sea level has increased by an average of more than 4.7 inches (12 cm) in the last century, Arctic sea ice has thinned by 40 percent in recent decades, and winter has shortened between one and four days per decade over the last 40 years.

Climate scientists predict that by the year 2100, the global mean surface temperature will have increased by somewhere between 2.5°F to 12.4°F (1.4°C to 5.8°C). Extreme weather conditions such as floods, droughts, and hurricanes are likely to become more commonplace, and rising sea levels will swamp vast areas of land.

Scientists predict that polar bears could become extinct by the end of the century. Their hunting grounds are being reduced as the sea ice thins, and they are having to swim farther to find food.

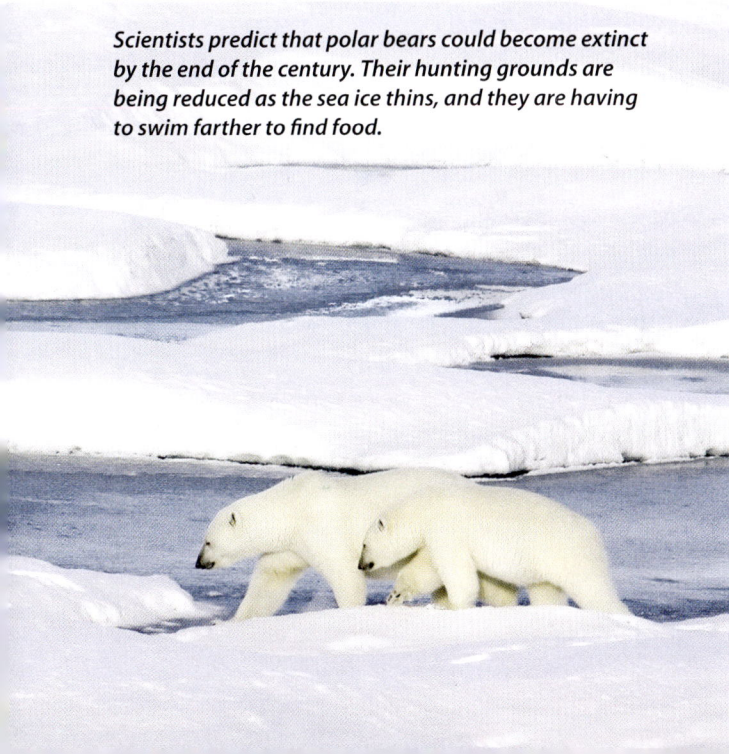

*❝ **Because greenhouse gases continue to increase, we are, in effect, conducting a global climate experiment, neither planned nor controlled, the results of which may present unprecedented challenges to our wisdom and foresight as well as have significant impacts on our natural and societal systems.** ❞*

Statement issued by the American Meteorological Society, 2003

YOU DECIDE

The U.S. has not signed the Kyoto Protocol (see page 16), but individual states such as California are taking the matter into their own hands by signing agreements to reduce greenhouse gases.

? *Who should take responsibility for reducing greenhouse gases: governments, states, or individuals?*

? *Is it fair for wealthy, developed nations to force developing countries such as China and India to reduce their emissions?*

? *Are agreements like the Kyoto Protocol the best way to tackle global warming, or will new technologies provide an answer?*

Garibaldi Secondary School
24789 Dewdney Trunk Road
Maple Ridge, B.C.
V4R 1X2

The Sizewell B nuclear power plant in the UK was built in the 1980s. Since then, there have been campaigns to shut it down.

POWER FACTS

■ *A coal-fired power plant releases more radioactivity into the environment than a nuclear power plant.*

■ *The energy in 1 pound (.45 Kg) of uranium equals 1,500 tons (131 t) of coal.*

■ *A typical 1,000 megawatt nuclear power plant (enough to power almost one million homes) produces around 33 tons (30 t)of high-level radioactive waste each year.*

A Nuclear Future?

Tackling global warming will probably mean significantly reducing the amount of fossil fuels we use. Although several alternatives are available, each of them raises a new set of ethical issues.

One potential substitute is nuclear energy. Nuclear energy is emitted when a neutron is absorbed into the nucleus of an atom and the atom splits into two lighter nuclei. This is known as nuclear fission and is the process that occurs inside nuclear power plants. The fuel used is the element uranium, which contains about three million times more energy than fossil fuels.

Around 17 percent of the world's electricity is supplied by nuclear power plants. Unlike fossil fuels, no greenhouse gases are produced when making nuclear energy, although the mining of uranium does result in some greenhouse-gas emissions. Another advantage of nuclear power is that uranium is a common element, found in most rocks and soils.

However, nuclear power plants are very expensive to build, and after nuclear accidents like the Chernobyl disaster in Ukraine

In nuclear fission, a neutron is fired at the nucleus of an element such as uranium. As the uranium nucleus splits, it produces energy in the form of heat. This is used to heat water, making steam, which in turn can power turbines.

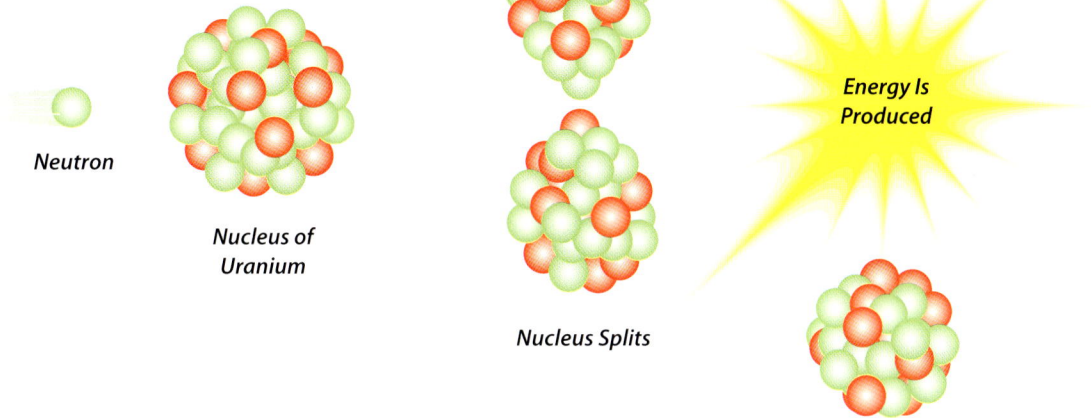

Energy Is Produced

Neutron

Nucleus of Uranium

Nucleus Splits

YOU DECIDE

One of the main concerns about nuclear power is how to store the waste. Most radioactive waste needs to be stored for 10,000 years or more—equivalent to more than 300 human generations.

? *Is using nuclear power fair to future generations, and should they have to worry about our waste?*

? *Should every country have to dispose of its own nuclear waste, or is it acceptable to trade nuclear waste between countries?*

? *Do the risks associated with nuclear power outweigh the risks posed by global warming?*

in 1986, many people are concerned about the safety of nuclear power. Like fossil fuels, uranium will run out eventually. Also, making nuclear power produces radioactive waste, some of which needs to be stored for many thousands of years before it becomes safe. Some people are concerned that this waste gets into the wrong hands, it could be used to make nuclear weapons.

Nuclear Fusion

Another option is nuclear fusion, the energy produced when nuclei crash into each other and fuse together. This is the same process that fuels stars, including our Sun. It keeps them burning, and it is an attractive way of making energy on Earth. Nuclear fusion produces huge amounts of energy, and there are no dangerous waste products or greenhouse gases.

However, it takes a lot of energy to get nuclear fusion started. So far, no one has found a way of creating energy from nuclear fusion on Earth. An international team of scientists is working on the problem, and plans are underway to build an experimental reactor (ITER) at Cadarache in the south of France to research ways of making nuclear-fusion reactions.

3 Renewable Resources

Renewable energy sources can be replenished as quickly as they are used. Wind, wave, solar, water, and geothermal power are all examples. They are often seen as a solution to debates about global warming and the environment. But are renewable resources really the answer, and can they provide enough power for everyone in the world?

In general, renewable energy produces very little pollution and is sustainable. Resources can be replaced as fast as they are used. Most forms of renewable energy produce few greenhouse gases, making them very important in the fight against global warming. Groups campaigning for greener energy sources encourage the use of those that are renewable, such as wind and water power.

However, there are problems with renewable resources too, both practical and ethical. Generally they are not as efficient as fossil fuels or nuclear power, and large areas of

Capturing some kinds of renewable energy requires large areas of land. Solar farms are a good example. The one pictured below is in California.

The Dinorwig power station in Wales is a pumped storage hydroelectric plant. Water is pumped to a reservoir at off-peak times and then released through turbines at peak times.

land have to be used to capture sufficient quantities of power. Also, many renewable energy technologies are expensive to build at the moment, although they might become cheaper if people start using them on a larger scale. Therefore, a big ethical debate is based around the monetary cost in relation to the cost to the environment.

Uneven Distribution of Energy

There is enough wind, sunshine, and water to provide power for everyone in the world, but these resources are not always readily available where they are needed. For example, there is lots of solar energy—energy from the Sun—in the Sahara Desert, but very few people live there.

Perhaps the biggest problem of all is intermittency. Wind turbines only provide power when the wind blows, for example. Conventional fossil fuels and nuclear power plants can control their output and increase production when necessary. When renewable resources are being used, people have to rely on pumped storage hydroelectric plants when there are surges in demand.

Decentralized Power

Pumped storage could fill some of the gaps for renewable resources, but other solutions would also be needed. Currently scientists are investigating ways of storing renewable energy in special batteries.

However, if renewable resources are to be taken seriously, global power-distribution systems must change. Unlike fossil fuels and nuclear energy, renewable resources work much more efficiently when they operate on a small scale. Less energy is lost as it is converted into power, and every community makes the best use of the renewable resources available to it. Making this kind of change in infrastructure would be expensive.

YOU DECIDE

Renewable power sources are not as efficient as fossil fuels or nuclear power, and at the moment they are more expensive to produce.

? *Should we be willing to accept these costs because of the long-term benefits of halting global warming?*

? *Would it be better to wait for more efficient renewable technologies to be developed, rather than facing the issues caused by wind turbines or solar panels?*

Wind farms provide clean energy from a renewable resource, but they also cause noise pollution and use up large tracts of land. Some argue that they are an unsightly addition to the landscape.

WIND FARMS

Although the U.S. has several important wind farms, currently less than 1 percent of its electricity comes from wind power. In Denmark, around 20 percent of electricity consumption is covered by electricity produced at wind farms. Wind turbines could provide 20 percent of America's electricity by covering just 1 percent of the land with wind farms.

Wind Energy

Antarctica is probably the windiest place in the world, but there is no need to go all the way to Antarctica to feel a breeze, because wind is everywhere. Traditionally, people have captured the wind's energy, using windmills to grind grain, pump water, and even saw wood. So can wind provide us with energy today?

Wind turbines gather energy from the wind and convert it into electricity. The three blades of the turbine are pushed around by the wind. This spins a shaft, connected to a generator that makes electricity.

A Clean Solution

The big advantage of wind energy is that it produces no greenhouse gases. There is also no air pollution or waste products, and once the turbine has been constructed, the energy source is free. Germany is currently the world's leading wind-power nation, followed by Spain and the U.S.

Places with strong, steady winds are best for wind turbines. Unfortunately, these windy places are often wilderness areas, which provide an important habitat for animals, birds, and plants. Some people are concerned that wind turbines could have a negative impact on the wildlife in these special environments. Others say that wind turbines are unsightly and spoil the countryside.

Harming Nature

In particular, the turbines can present a threat to birds and bats, especially if a wind farm is situated on a bird migratory route. Plants and animals can also suffer during the construction phase when new roads are built to transport the turbines to their sites, and large amounts of concrete are used to support them. Some of these environmental impacts can be avoided by erecting the wind farms out at sea, but this is more costly. Are these small prices to pay for the human and environmental benefits of wind energy?

The construction of wind farms in places where rare birds like the golden eagle are still found is causing concern among some groups of people. They fear that the destruction of the birds' habitats may result in them dying out altogether.

66 *Wind farms must be located away from narrow bird migration routes and important feeding, breeding, and roosting areas. They must not be permitted where they would have adverse impacts on nationally and internationally protected wildlife sites.* **99**

Royal Society for the Protection of Birds

Water Power

Water is one of the most powerful forces of nature, and scientists are now looking at water power as a possible alternative to energy from nonrenewable resources. Crashing waves, tidal cycles, gushing rivers, and reservoirs are all full of energy. High-level lakes contain a lot of potential, or stored, energy. Hydroelectric power plants provide one way of capturing this energy, by releasing a controlled flow of water from an upper reservoir to a lower level. The water turns a turbine on the way.

Mountains and Rain

Countries such as China, Canada, Austria, Norway, and Scotland, have plenty of rainfall, mountains, and valleys that are ideal places for hydroelectric plants. It is a relatively cheap source of energy, and it is renewable. In addition, using hydroelectric power overcomes the intermittency problem by storing water when it rains and slowly releasing the energy as it is needed.

Most of the best sites for hydroelectric power plants have already been used in developed nations, but in developing countries there is room to build more large-scale plants. The ethical questions about the use of water power surround the damage that can be caused to the environment by the construction of such plants. Blocking a river with a large concrete dam provides a barrier to fish and causes silt to build up. Many animals, plants, and people can also lose their homes when a valley is flooded.

The Jochenstein hydroelectric power plant lies on the River Danube between Austria and Germany. Countries such as these are well suited to using hydroelectric power plants, because they have relatively high levels of rainfall.

HYDROELECTRICITY

■ *Around 20 percent of the world's electricity is generated by hydroelectric power.*

■ *In 1975, a typhoon caused 62 dams in China's Henan Province to fail. An estimated 26,000 people died from the flooding and nearly 6 million buildings collapsed.*

■ *If 0.1 percent of the energy of the oceans were converted to electricity, it would be enough to supply the world's energy demand more than five times over.*

The Pelamis Wave Energy Converter has been used in a "wave farm" constructed in 2006 off the coast of Portugal. It converts the energy of surface waves on the ocean into electricity.

YOU DECIDE

When it is fully operational in 2009, the Three Gorges Dam in China will be the largest in the world. More than one million people have already been displaced by the building of the dam, and many archeological and cultural sites will be flooded. It will supply less than three percent of China's electricity needs.

? *How should the displaced people be compensated for their loss of housing and land, and who should pay for this?*

? *Is it safe to build such a large dam, especially in a country that suffers from earthquakes? Would you live downstream from this dam?*

? *Is it fair for developed nations to criticize this dam, when they have already benefited from building large hydroelectric plants?*

Waves and Tides

Gathering energy from the ocean is another option. The push and pull of the Moon sucks the oceans in and out twice a day, moving vast amounts of water. This movement creates energy. The challenge is working out how to capture these forms of energy. Scientists and engineers are working hard to solve this problem, and there are now several wave and tidal plants in operation in countries such as France and Canada. Japan also has a program to find ways of harnessing wave energy to provide power to coastal communities. However, at the moment, the cost of building tidal plants is preventing large-scale development.

Solar Power

Solar power is one of the most abundant sources of renewable energy. On average, the Sun provides around 200 watts of energy per square yard (.83m²), enough to power roughly two lightbulbs. However, the debates surrounding the use of solar energy are similar to those about other renewable resources. In order to capture enough energy to make it viable, large areas of land need to be used. Possible consequences include damage to natural habitats and the displacement of people.

Solar-Energy Factories

There are several ways of gathering solar energy. Solar panels on the roofs of buildings focus the Sun's rays and use them to heat water in pipes underneath. Photovoltaic cells are similar, but these special cells have a more sophisticated technology that turns the Sun's heat into an electric current, which can be used to power the home.

Solar energy can also be captured on a larger scale. The largest solar plant in the world is in the Mojave Desert at Kramer Junction, California. Its banks of curving, shiny mirrors concentrate sunlight and heat a fluid, which is used to make steam that turns a turbine and generates electricity.

In Australia there are plans to build a .62 mile (1 km) high "solar tower." The Sun's warmth will heat air, which will then rise through the tower and spin turbines, creating power.

This solar power tower is at the Barstow power plant in California. Mirrors at the bottom of the tower focus the Sun's rays onto a receiver at the top, which creates steam from the heat. The steam is used to power turbines, generating electricity.

Percentage

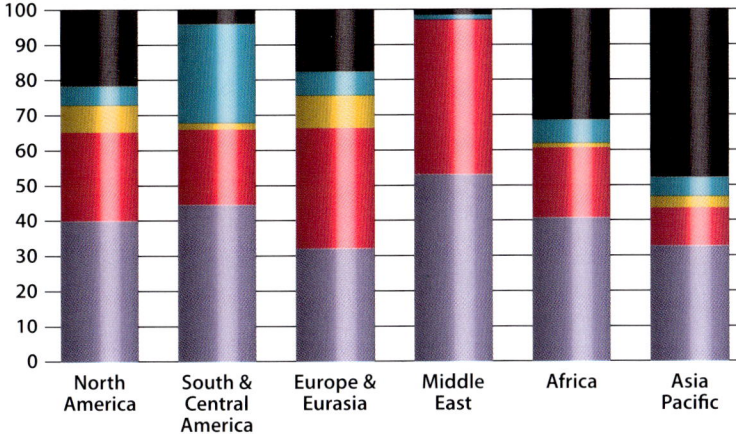

This graph shows the relative amounts of energy used in different parts of the world. Nonrenewable resources still make up the majority of energy sources all over the globe.

● Oil
● Natural gas
● Nuclear energy
● Hydroelectricity
● Coal

Down Below

Heat can also come from deep underground. The temperature at the center of the Earth is around 9,932°F (5,500°C), about the same as it is on the surface of the Sun. Volcanic countries, such as Iceland, have a superhighway to this heat source and can tap into it by piping up the water from hot springs. This can be used directly to heat houses, or indirectly, using steam to drive a turbine and make electricity.

Nonvolcanic countries can also make use of the Earth's heat. Although not as hot as the volcanic areas, the upper 9.8 feet (3 m) of the Earth's surface have a constant temperature of around (50°F to 60.8°F (10°C to16°C). Special heat pumps absorb the heat from below by piping water down to around 60 feet (20 m) and then pumping it back up again. For every unit of electricity used to pump the heat, three to four units of heat are produced. When renewable energy powers the pump, it offers a truly green solution.

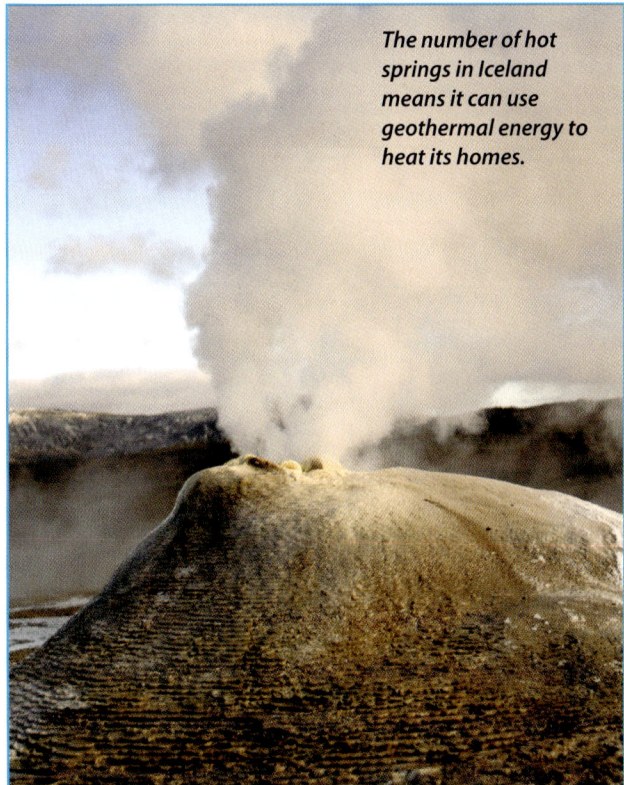

The number of hot springs in Iceland means it can use geothermal energy to heat its homes.

GEOTHERMAL ENERGY

In Reykjavik, Iceland, more than 95 percent of the buildings are heated with geothermal water pumped from deep wells. Geothermal energy is an environmentally friendly solution. It is not suitable everywhere, because installing the system involves disrupting building foundations and surrounding land.

4 Transportation and Travel

The world has opened up dramatically over the past few decades. Now, thanks to cars, boats, airplanes, trains, and buses, we can travel farther, more frequently, and in greater comfort than ever before. This globalization in transportation and travel has raised several serious ethical questions about the effects it is having on natural resources and the environment.

In large cities such as Los Angeles, a permanent smog hangs in the air from pollution caused by traffic emissions.

Many countries are now encouraging people to bicycle by creating special bike lanes along the roads.

Transportation Pollution

Almost all the forms of transportation we use are powered by fossil fuels, especially oil. Vehicles need an energy source that is stable (not dangerously explosive or flammable), portable, lightweight, high energy, and that can be turned on or off at will. Gasoline is ideal. It is relatively stable, easily transportable, packed full of energy, and easy to stop and start. This convenience comes at a cost, though. Burning oil in engines produces greenhouse gases as well as a cocktail of other chemicals that are damaging to health. Carbon monoxide, nitrogen monoxide, benzene, lead, and tiny particles are just some of the damaging products that can result in health problems.

Much of modern life depends on transportation—and not just for vacations. Food, clothes, and almost everything else people use require some form of transportation to get them to retail outlets. In developed countries, nearly 40 percent of energy consumption is due to transportation.

A Growing Problem

The issues surrounding the use of natural resources in travel and transportation are causing increasing alarm in many countries. In 2004, people in the U.S. covered over 2.9 trillion passenger miles (4.8 trillion passenger km)—or 10,055 miles (16,181 km) per person. Approximately 99% of that traveling was by road. In 1960, people in the U.S. covered 722 billion passenger miles (1,162 billion passenger km)—or 4,036 miles (6,495 km) per person. So the average of miles traveled per person in 2004 is two and one-half times the 1960 average. Traveling has become faster and more affordable, tempting us to travel more. Whether for vacations in exotic locations, commuting longer distances to work, or simply driving to the store instead of walking, we are continually on the move. Just because it is easier and more convenient to use transportation, should we be ignoring the effect it is having on the environment?

YOU DECIDE

Traveling by car, boat, plane, or train produces greenhouse-gas emissions and other pollutants that are bad for health and the environment.

? *Do we need to travel as much as we do?*

? *Would you consider traveling less, or using less polluting transport (for example, a bicycle instead of a car) for the sake of the environment?*

? *Should the government discourage people from traveling by taxing transportation more heavily?*

Air Travel

Some forms of transportation pollute more than others, and this is an area in which every individual can make ethical decisions that will affect the Earth's future.

For example, flying might be a convenient and fast way of getting around, but it is one of the most environmentally damaging methods of transportation. Aircraft have a greater impact on climate change than ground transportation. The water vapor in aircraft exhaust creates clouds or contrails, which intercept sunlight and change the temperature of the atmosphere. Add to this the 771 million tons (700 million t) of carbon dioxide emitted by commercial aircraft every year, and you have a recipe for global warming.

Aircraft can also cause problems at ground level. Takeoff and landing can cause noise pollution, and usually acres of countryside are lost for runways.

Studies over the past 10 years have shown that aircraft contrails are likely to be a contributing factor to global warming.

> **Increased cirrus [cloud] coverage, attributable to air traffic, could account for nearly all of the warming observed over the United States for nearly 20 years… Human activity has a visible and significant impact on cloud cover and, therefore, on climate. It indicates that contrails should be included in climate change scenarios.**

Patrick Minnis
Scientist, NASA's Langley Research Center

CARBON NEUTRALITY

In some countries, including Holland and the UK, programs have been introduced to help individuals gain "carbon credits." Each time you take a flight, you donate money to an organization such as Trees for Life or Trees for Travel. This money is used to plant trees, which absorb carbon dioxide. This is a way to help neutralize the effects of pollution caused by air travel.

SUVs emit significantly more carbon dioxide than ordinary cars. Some special interest groups are campaigning to ban the use of SUVs in towns and cities.

Personal Cars

In most developed countries a high percentage of the population owns a private car. A car gives us the freedom to move around wherever and whenever we want, and to carry passengers and goods from one place to another. Like aircraft, though, personal cars are heavy contributors to global warming and atmospheric pollution.

The average car produces around 4.4 tons (4 t) of carbon dioxide each year. Drive a gas-guzzling SUV, and this can easily triple to around 13.2 tons (12 t) of carbon dioxide per year. In busy cities such as Los Angeles, vehicle emissions can create a toxic smog that is bad for people's health and the environment.

Public Transportation

Traveling on a public train, bus, or boat tends to be less damaging to the environment because the journey and resulting emissions are shared among many people. On average, using public transportation can reduce emissions by two-thirds or more compared to traveling in a car. However, in many countries the systems of public transportation are not widespread, reliable, or cheap enough to convince people to use them instead of their private cars.

YOU DECIDE

Although air travel is the quickest way of traveling, it is extremely damaging to the environment. It might take longer to travel by boat, for example, but such methods cause far less pollution.

? *Would you consider alternative methods of transportation when you go on vacation?*

? *Should airlines have to pay a tax on their fuel?*

? *How could such a tax be implemented globally?*

The growing market for palm oil as a biofuel is encouraging Indonesians to cut down tropical forest, reducing the habitat for endangered species such as the orangutan.

Biofuels

Several ethical alternatives to polluting fuels are being developed. Filling a gas tank with turkey guts might sound unpleasant, but it could be a "green" alternative to oil. A biofuel is any fuel from a recently living organism (such as a tree) or its by-product (such as turkey guts or manure from cows). These are renewable and could help reduce greenhouse gases. Compared to fossil fuels, which locked up carbon from millions of years ago, plants and trees captured their carbon more recently, so burning them does not result in an overall increase of carbon dioxide in the atmosphere.

Many plants can be used to produce "bioethanol" and "biodiesel" alternatives to gasoline and diesel for road transportation. Ordinary cars can run on a blend of 5 percent biofuel and 95 percent gasoline. Meanwhile, making a few changes to the engine enables vehicles to run on pure ethanol.

Converting cars to run on biofuel would be relatively painless and easy to do. However, growing biofuels can be damaging for the environment, especially if tropical forests are cut down to make space for biofuel fields. Moreover, biofuel still contributes to air pollution, and it cannot be used in aircraft yet.

YOU DECIDE

One possible way of encouraging people to travel less would be to introduce a "carbon credits" program. Each time you fill the car with gas, take a flight, or even turn the heating up a notch at home, you would use up some of your carbon quota. At the end of the year, those people who have a surplus of carbon credits, could sell them to those people who have run out.

? *Is it fair to ration carbon in this way?*

? *Should everyone be given the same carbon quota or should some people be allowed more, such as someone who lives in a very cold country, for example?*

Hydrogen

Another possible solution to the transportation problem is hydrogen. This can be burned like oil or reacted with oxygen inside a "fuel cell" to produce electricity. However, unlike fossil and nuclear fuels, hydrogen cannot be mined; it has to be made. It can be produced from hydrocarbons such as methane, or extracted from water using electrolysis, a process that uses a lot of energy. With a few very expensive exceptions (like wind- or water-powered electrolysis), these procedures produce greenhouse gases.

Even if it were possible to find a cheap and clean way to produce hydrogen, it would be costly and difficult to convert everyone's cars and homes to run on hydrogen. Is this really a viable option?

Hydrogen fuel-cell cars are very clean, emitting only heat and water from their exhausts. They are also more efficient, offering two to three times higher mileage on equivalent energy. It is possible to buy hydrogen cars now, but they are very expensive.

5 Wood and Water

Energy is not the only natural resource that humans use in large quantities. Water, timber, rocks, and minerals are all vital, too. For example, most people live in houses made of stone, brick, or wood. Every day we drink and wash with water. Overuse of these resources can threaten the environment.

Nearly three-fourths of the world is covered in water, but almost all of it is salty. Only three percent of the water on Earth is fresh. Two-thirds of this is locked up in ice caps and glaciers. Water is probably the most precious resource on Earth, and yet most people are very wasteful about how they use it. The average American uses around 100 gallons (380 l) of water every day—more than enough to make a bathtub overflow. Most of this water is flushed down the toilet, sprinkled on the yard, or used to wash the car.

The processes of evaporation and rainfall keep water on the move around the world. However, the distribution of freshwater around the globe is not evenly balanced.

Where Does Water Come From?

Some of our water comes from reservoirs and lakes, which are replenished by rainfall. The remainder is usually groundwater, which has trickled through cracks in the Earth and is pumped up from deep underground. Some groundwater has been lying beneath the surface of the Earth for thousands of years.

Water is moved around the Earth by the processes of evaporation and rainfall. However, the rain does not fall evenly, and some places get much more than they need while others remain parched. As the world's population grows and lifestyles in many countries improve, water consumption increases. Sometimes there just isn't enough water to go around.

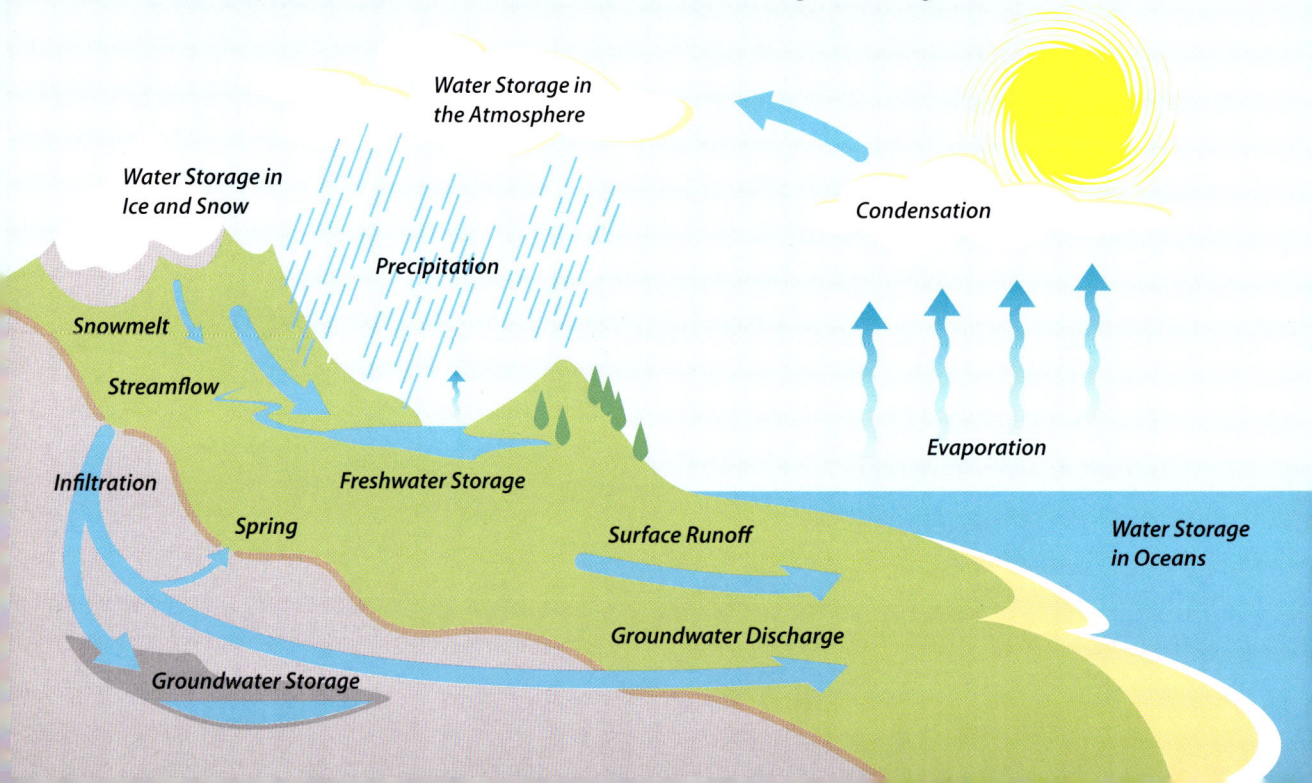

Water Storage in the Atmosphere

Water Storage in Ice and Snow

Condensation

Precipitation

Snowmelt

Streamflow

Evaporation

Infiltration

Freshwater Storage

Spring

Surface Runoff

Water Storage in Oceans

Groundwater Discharge

Groundwater Storage

Today, rusting fishing boats lie scattered on dry land in what was once the Aral Sea, and the seashore is more than 62 miles (100 km) away.

The Disappearing Sea

Aralsk, a small city in southwestern Kazakhstan, used to be a thriving fishing port, sitting on the banks of the Aral Sea in central Asia. During the last 50 years, the sea has shrunk to less than half its original area. The water that is left is very salty and most of the fish have died. People living in the area suffer from lack of fresh water and health problems due to the toxic dust that blows up from what was once the seabed. Water that would have once gushed into the Aral Sea is now diverted to irrigate crops, such as rice, melon, cereals, and cotton in Kazakhstan and Uzbekistan.

Conflict over water use is likely to become worse in the future. Climate changes are predicted to bring more extreme weather such as floods and droughts. A recent World Water Development Report estimated that by 2050, at least one in four people is likely to live in a country affected by chronic freshwater shortage.

WATER USAGE
Irrigation accounts for around 70 percent of global water usage. Industry uses 15 percent, while the remaining 15 percent goes to household use.

YOU DECIDE

Producing 2.2 pounds (1 kg) of bananas requires 105.6 gallons (400 l) of water, but 2.2 pounds (1 kg) of tomatoes needs just 10.5 gallons (40 l). Over the last 40 years, the River Jordan has been reduced to a trickle as farmers in Israel, Syria, Jordan and Palestine divert the water to irrigate tropical crops such as bananas.

? *Should people be allowed to grow water-thirsty crops in countries such as Israel, where there is not enough rain and they rely on irrigation?*

? *How can—and should—other countries intervene?*

? *Would you buy a banana that had been grown in the Israeli desert?*

Trees and the Environment

For thousands of years, humans have been building things from wood. Even today, with many new materials available, wood products can still be seen everywhere—books, magazines, tables, doors, even whole buildings. Wood might be extremely useful to humans, but the trees from which wood comes also play an important part in environmental balance. Trees and plants take in carbon dioxide from the atmosphere and give out oxygen, providing us with fresh air to breathe. In addition, they help keep the air clean by absorbing some of the pollutants from power plants, industry, and cars. The rate at which trees are being cut down is now a matter of grave concern to environmentalists.

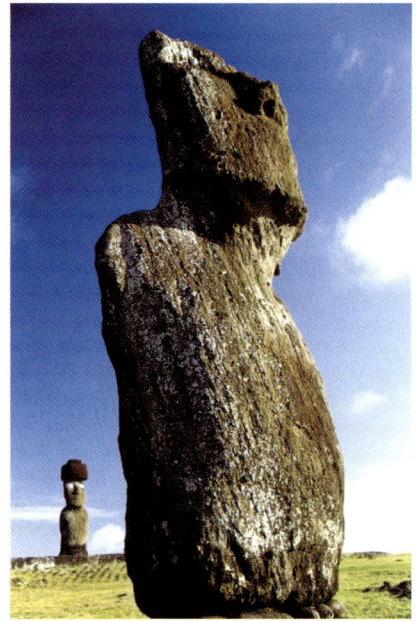

Some archeologists think that the Easter Islanders deforested their island between A.D. 1200 and A.D. 1500 in order to erect statues such as this one.

YOU DECIDE

The island of Tasmania is home to some of the world's tallest and oldest trees, but these are rapidly disappearing as the trees are cut. Logging is an important industry in Tasmania, providing more than 7,000 people with jobs.

? *Should other countries be preventing Tasmania from cutting down its trees?*

? *Do we have a right to stop people from doing what they want with their natural resources?*

? *Is there a way that Tasmania could keep its trees without adversely affecting local people and economies?*

Clearing the Land

Easter Island is a remote island in the Pacific Ocean, which has been inhabited for around 1,500 years. Around 500 years ago, the people suffered a catastrophe when they ran out of trees. They could no longer make boats to go fishing, and the deforestation led to soil erosion, making it difficult to grow crops. The few people that survived are thought to have resorted to cannibalism.

The problem of deforestation has grown dramatically in recent years. Currently we are cutting down trees faster than we can replace them. When these trees are cut down or burned, they release carbon back into the atmosphere and contribute to global warming.

One reason for deforestation is to make space for farmland. In the Amazon rain forest in Brazil, farmers have cleared the trees in order to grow soybeans and raise cattle. Brazil is now the world's biggest exporter of beef, and the ranchers are growing rich. In the process, however, native people have lost their homes and livelihoods, plants and animals have become extinct, and global temperatures have continued to rise. Already nearly one-fifth of Brazil's rain forest has disappeared.

June 17, 2002

June 28, 2006

These satellite images show how much of Brazil's rain forest has been cut down in just four years. If cutting continues at this rate, scientists estimate that the Amazon rain forest will have disappeared by 2050.

The map on the right shows the difference in deforested areas between 2002 and 2006. The largest cleared areas are red, areas that had no forest in 2002 are white, and areas that were still forested in 2006 are gray.

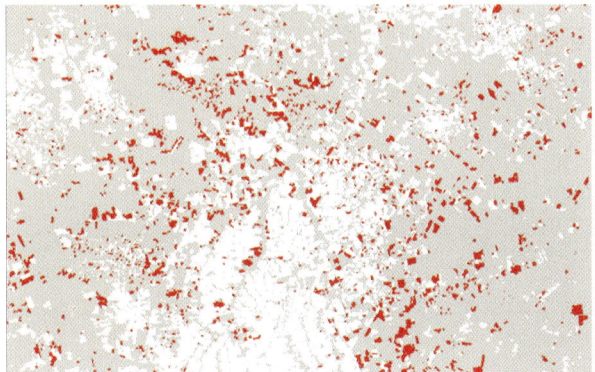

6 The Environment and You

The way we choose to live our lives can have a huge impact on the environment and its resources. Below are some examples of the different lifestyles people enjoy, and the ways in which our actions affect the environment every day.

Joe

Joe Planter is 15 years old and lives in San Francisco with his mother, father, sister Kim, and dog Dudley. When he is not at school, Joe likes to go skateboarding and mountain biking with his friends, and listens to music on his iPod. He also supports his local basketball team, the Golden State Warriors, watching matches at home on the family's giant plasma TV.

Joe and Kim catch the bus to school each day, taking a packed lunch made by Mrs. Planter. The Planters are all vegetarian, but Joe sometimes sneaks a burger when he is out with his friends. When Joe gets home from school, he walks Dudley, usually in Golden Gate Park. On weekends the family loads up the car, an SUV, with bikes and heads off to Marin County for a ride. Every winter the family goes skiing for a week in Yosemite National Park. In summer they usually take a vacation along the California coast.

Driving an SUV can cause much more damage to the environment than driving an ordinary car.

38

> **❝ The ultimate test of man's conscience may be his willingness to sacrifice something today for future generations whose words of thanks will not be heard. ❞**
>
> *Gaylord Nelson*
> *Cofounder of Earth Day*

Fieke

Fieke Van Rijn is 14 years old and lives with her mother, father, and two sisters on a cheese farm near the town of Uithoorn in the Netherlands. Each day the girls get a lift to school in Mr. Van Rijn's cheese van, after which he delivers his cheese to the stores. In her spare time Fieke likes to ride horses and sometimes enters competitions on her pony, Nassau.

As well as eating the cheese made on their farm, the Van Rijns grow their own vegetables and buy their meat from the local butcher. On weekends, the Van Rijns usually relax at home or load the horses into their horse trailer and drive to an event. Every summer Mr. Van Rijn's brother comes to look after the farm and the family enjoys a two-week vacation. Last year they went on a safari in Kenya. This year they are going to climb Mount Fuji in Japan.

YOU DECIDE

Joe and Fieke lead very different lifestyles, but which is better?

? *What kind of impact do they each have on the environment, who uses the most resources, and who creates the most pollution?*

? *Joe and his family eat a lot of soy (grown in the Amazon) and buy imported fruit and vegetables. Fieke's family eats homegrown vegetables and locally raised meat. What kind of impact do these different diets have on the environment? Can being vegetarian help save resources and energy?*

? *What kind of changes could Joe and Fieke make in their lives to reduce their greenhouse-gas emissions from travel?*

Buying food from a local farm, or even making or growing it yourself, has many environmental advantages over shopping at the supermarket.

Old versus New

It is not just governments and scientists who need to address the ethical questions surrounding the use of natural resources and the environment. These are issues that everyone can act on. What kind of impact do you, your family, and your friends have on the environment? Could you change your lifestyle and use fewer natural resources?

How old is your refrigerator at home? If it is more than 10 years old, then it probably uses much more electricity than a newer model. Would it be better to replace it with a new one? Older refrigerators sometimes consume more than three times as much energy as new, energy-efficient models. But keeping your food cool is only half the picture. What about the energy it took to obtain the raw materials and build the refrigerator before it reached your home?

When replacing old items such as cars, refrigerators, washing machines, computers, and mobile phones, it is important to consider the whole life cycle of the object and ensure that the old models are recycled properly.

Recycling is one of the main ways in which individuals can help save energy. In this recycling plant in Germany, electrical devices from mobile phones to freezers can be recycled.

Organic versus Local

Growing plants organically means that chemical fertilizers, pesticides, and herbicides are not used, and the farming tends to be less mechanized. Generally this is good for wildlife and encourages a greater diversity of species. However, the yield from an organic farm is usually less, meaning that more land would need to be farmed if everyone in the world ate organic food.

Another consideration is how far the food has traveled to reach your plate. Is it better to buy organic green beans from Kenya or nonorganic green beans from a farm just down the road?

Nonorganic farming provides higher yields but can be detrimental to plants and wildlife.

Turn Out the Light

Sometimes very small changes can make a big difference if everyone does them. Leaving televisions and other gadgets on standby wastes huge amounts of energy. Meanwhile, taking a bath instead of a shower can use up to five times as much water. These are areas in which the dilemmas can be resolved with the help of every individual.

If you live in Scotland, is it better to buy local tomatoes that have been grown in heated greenhouses, or imported Spanish tomatoes that grew under the sun?

YOU DECIDE

Making small changes in everyday habits could have a big effect on resources and the environment if everyone took responsibility.

? *Is it right to impose changes such as carpooling, compulsory recycling, and water restrictions (watering bans during drought, for example)?*

? *Can voluntary individual action make a significant difference, or should we wait until governments force us to change our ways?*

Time Line

1962
Rachel Carson publishes *Silent Spring*.

1969
Friends of the Earth is founded.

1970
The first Earth Day is held, and millions of people all over the world demonstrate in favor of cleaning up the environment.

1979
The Three Mile Island nuclear power plant in the U.S. partially melts down. James Lovelock publishes the Gaia theory.

1982
The World Resources Institute is founded in the U.S. to find ways of managing global resources without compromising human needs.

1986
Explosions at the nuclear power plant in Chernobyl, Ukraine, create the world's worst nuclear power accident. Immediately 31 people die and shortly after 200 become seriously ill from the effects of the radiation. Experts estimate that more than 8,000 people die from diseases caused by the radiation over the next 8 years.

1989
The oil tanker *Exxon Valdez* runs aground in Alaska, spilling millions of gallons of oil, threatening wildlife.

1991
The United Nations Antarctic Treaty comes into effect, banning mining and limiting pollution in the Antarctic region.

1992
The Earth Summit is held in Brazil, focusing on helping developing countries find ways of adopting environmentally friendly processes, and discussing issues such as rates of deforestation and climate change.

2000
The European Union bans the use of leaded gasoline.

2002
The German government announces that it plans to increase its wind generation over the next 25 years. The World Summit on Sustainable Development is held in South Africa.

2005
The Kyoto Protocol comes into effect. Those countries which ratified the agreement have committed to reducing carbon emissions in their countries.

2006
Greenpeace activists try to prevent the unloading of a coal shipment in Thailand.

2007
Construction begins on the experimental reactor (ITER) at Cadarache in the south of France to research ways of making nuclear-fusion reactions.

More Information

● Books

The Ages of Gaia by James Lovelock, Oxford University Press, 2000

Climate Change Begins at Home: Life on the Two-Way Street of Global Warming
by Dave Reay, Palgrave Macmillan, 2006

The Earth's Resources by Richard and Louise Spilsbury, Evans Brothers, 2006

An Inconvenient Truth: The Crisis in Global Warming by Al Gore, Viking Juvenile, 2007

Save Energy, Save the Planet by Claire Llewellyn, Chrysalis Books, 2005

Silent Spring by Rachel Carson, Penguin Books, 2000

Sustainable Development by Clive Gifford, Heinemann Library, 2004

● Web sites

www.greenpeace.org/international/ Greenpeace.

www.earthday.net/default.aspx Earth Day Network.

www.foei.org/ Friends of the Earth.

www.heritage.org/ The Heritage Foundation.

www.aim.org/ Accuracy in Media.

www.sepp.org/ Science and Environmental Policy Project.

www.eia.doe.gov/ Energy Information Administration.

www.coolkidsforacoolclimate.com/ Cool Kids for a Cool Climate.

http://www.bbc.co.uk/climate
BBC climate change.

www.awea.org/ American Wind Energy Association.

www.nrel.gov/wind/ National Wind Technology Center.

www.chooseclimate.org/ Choose Climate – a website to calculate your own emissions.

www.changingworldtech.com/ Changing World Technologies (the company that converts turkey waste into fuel).

www.ran.org/ Rainforest Action Network.

www.carbontrust.co.uk/default.ct The Carbon Trust.

Glossary

biofuel fuel that is made from a recently living organism or its by-products.

civilization advanced human society where people live in cities and get their food from agriculture.

contrail artificial cloud produced by the condensation trail from the exhaust of an aircraft engine.

deforestation cutting down trees and converting forested areas to nonforested areas.

electrolysis method of breaking the bonds in elements and compounds by passing an electric current through them.

ethics a formalized set of rules generally developed from widely held morals. Ethical codes may become accepted by an entire society, then they often develop into laws (*see* morals).

evaporation process where atoms or molecules gain energy and change from being in a liquid state to a gaseous state.

fossil fuel fuel formed in the past from fossils, the remains of animals and plants.

Gaia theory named after a Greek goddess, Gaia theory was proposed by British scientist James Lovelock and suggests that the Earth behaves as if it were a living organism.

globalization operating on a global scale.

global warming gradual rise in temperature of the Earth's atmosphere, caused by the burning of fossil fuels.

greenhouse gas atmospheric gas that absorbs infrared radiation from the Sun and helps keep the Earth warm.

groundwater water located beneath the ground, in cracks, pores, and fractures within soil or rocks.

hydroelectric energy energy captured from moving water.

incineration burning of solid waste material.

Industrial Revolution major change in technological, economic, and social conditions that began in the late eighteenth century in Britain and spread throughout the world.

intermittent not continuous.

irrigation supplying water to crops and plants to supplement or replace rainfall water.

kinetic energy energy arising from movement.

Kyoto Protocol agreement made under the United Nations Framework Convention on Climate Change (UNFCCC), which commits signatories to reduce their emissions of carbon dioxide and five other greenhouse gases, or engage in emissions trading if they maintain or increase emissions of these gases.

landfill method of disposing of solid waste material, in which it is crushed and spread out across a special site, then covered with soil.

morals a set of beliefs held by an individual. Morals may come from religious beliefs or the values of the individual (*see* ethics).

nuclear energy Energy released from the nucleus of an atom.

organic farming method of farming that severely restricts the use of artificial chemical fertilizers and pesticides on crops, and raises animals without the routine use of drugs, antibiotics, and wormers common in intensive livestock farming.

passenger miles (km) total distance traveled annually by passengers by all modes of transportation.

pesticide chemical sprayed on crops to kill pests that might destroy them.

photosynthesis process used by plants in which energy from sunlight is used to convert water and carbon dioxide into oxygen.

photovoltaic cell device that generates electricity when it is exposed to light.

pollutant substance that harms the environment when it mixes with soil, water, or air.

potential energy stored energy that results from the position or state of an object.

reservoir area where water is stored and regulated, ready to be used when there is a shortage.

resource (natural) naturally occurring substance that is considered valuable.

smog fog that is intensified by smoke or pollution. The word originates from a blend of the words "smoke" and "fog."

sustainable development harvesting resources no faster than they can be replaced.

SUV (Sports Utility Vehicle) a vehicle that combines features of a passenger car and a pickup truck.

zoologist scientist who studies animal biology.

Index

activists 9
air travel 30, 31
animals 14, 15, 23
Antarctica 22
Aral Sea 35
Arctic National Wildlife Refuge 15

biofuels 10, 11, 32
birds 8, 15, 23
Branson, Richard 10
Brazil 36, 37

Canada 24, 25
carbon capture 15
carbon credits 30, 32
carbon dioxide 15, 16, 17, 30, 31,
   32, 36
carbon monoxide 29
cars 12, 28, 31, 32, 33, 36
Carson, Rachel 8
Chernobyl disaster 18–19
China 24, 25
climate change 15, 17, 30, 35
coal 6, 7, 13, 14, 15, 18

dams 13, 24, 25
deforestation 36
Denmark 10, 22
droughts 17, 35, 41

Earth Day Network 8
Easter Island 36
electricity 13, 18, 22, 25, 27, 33
energy 12–19, 21, 22, 24, 25, 26, 27,
   29, 33, 34
energy efficiency 12, 40
European Union 10

floods 17, 35
forests 7, 32, 36, 37
fossil fuels 14–15, 18, 19, 20, 21, 29,
   32, 33

France 19, 25
Friends of the Earth 8

Gaia theory 9, 10
gas 6, 13, 14, 15
gasoline 12, 29, 32
geothermal power 20, 27
Germany 10, 22, 40
global warming 10, 11, 15, 17, 18,
   21, 30, 31, 36
globalization 7, 28
governments 6, 11, 15, 17, 29,
   40, 41
greenhouse gases 11, 16, 17, 18,
   19, 20, 22, 29, 32, 33, 39
Greenpeace 8, 9

Heritage Foundation 11
hydroelectricity 24, 25
hydrogen 13, 33

Industrial Revolution 7, 16
intermittency 21, 24

kinetic energy 13
Kyoto Protocol 16, 17

landfill 10
Lovelock, James 9

methane 16, 33
minerals 6, 34
mining 7, 11, 15, 18

nonrenewable resources 13, 15, 24
nuclear energy 18–19, 21

oil 6, 11, 13, 14, 15, 29, 32, 33
organic food 41
oxygen 9, 16, 17, 33, 36

pesticides 8, 41
plants 6, 14, 16, 17, 23, 36, 40
pollutants 15, 29, 32, 36
pollution 20, 22, 29, 30, 31, 32, 39
potential energy 13, 24
power plants 13, 15, 18, 36
pumped storage hydroelectric
   plants 21

radioactivity 15, 18, 19
recycling 10, 40, 41
renewable resources 13, 20–27, 32
reservoirs 24, 34

Scientific Alliance 11
solar power 11, 13, 20, 21, 26
special interest groups 6, 8, 11
Sun 6, 13, 19, 21, 26, 27
sustainable development 8, 20
SUVs 31, 38

technology 7, 17, 21, 26
tidal power 24, 25
transportation 28–33
trees 6, 16, 17, 30, 32, 36, 37

United Kingdom 11, 30
United States 11, 15, 17, 22, 29
uranium 13, 18, 19

Virgin Fuels 10
volcanoes 16, 27

water 6, 21, 24–25, 33, 34, 35
water power 24–25
water vapor 16, 30
wave power 13, 20, 24, 25
wildlife 8, 23, 41
wind power 6, 11, 13, 20, 21, 22–23
wind turbines 21, 22, 23
wood 34, 36